BOA
EDITIONS LTD

HOLY MOLY CARRY ME

Holy Moly Carry Me

POEMS BY

Erika Meitner

• • •

American Poets Continuum Series, no. 166

BOA Editions, Ltd. • Rochester, NY • 2018

For information about permission to reuse any material from this book, please contact The Permissions Company at www.permissionscompany.com or e-mail permdude@gmail.com.

Publications by BOA Editions, Ltd.—a not-for-profit corporation under section 501 (c) (3) of the United States Internal Revenue Code—are made possible with funds from a variety of sources, including public funds from the Literature Program of the National Endowment for the Arts; the New York State Council on the Arts, a state agency; and the County of Monroe, NY. Private funding sources include the Lannan Foundation; the Max and Marian Farash Charitable Foundation; the Mary S. Mulligan Charitable Trust; the Rochester Area Community Foundation; the Ames-Amzalak Memorial Trust in memory of Henry Ames, Semon Amzalak, and Dan Amzalak; and contributions from many individuals nationwide. See Colophon on page 108 for special individual acknowledgments.

ART WORKS.
arts.gov

State of the Arts

NYSCA

Cover Design: Sandy Knight
Cover Art: "Armagarden" by Jeff Gibson
Interior Design and Composition: Richard Foerster
Manufacturing: Bookmobile
BOA Logo: Mirko

Library of Congress Cataloging-in-Publication Data

Names: Meitner, Erika, 1975–
Title: Holy moly carry me : poems / by Erika Meitner.
Description: First edition. | Rochester, NY : BOA Editions, Ltd., 2018. |
  Series: American poets continuum series ; No. 166
Identifiers: LCCN 2018014184 (print) | LCCN 2018019301 (ebook) | ISBN
  9781942683636 (ebook) | ISBN 9781942683629 (pbk. : alk. paper)
Classification: LCC PS3613.E436 (ebook) | LCC PS3613.E436 A6 2018 (print) |
  DDC 811/.6—dc23
LC record available at https://lccn.loc.gov/2018014184

BOA Editions, Ltd.
250 North Goodman Street, Suite 306
Rochester, NY 14607
www.boaeditions.org
A. Poulin, Jr., Founder (1938–1996)

Contents

9   HolyMolyLand
17 Austerity
19 Medium / Message
22 Continuation
25 Hat Trick
28 Double Sonnet Ending in New Testament
29 On the Road
32 Diaspora
34 Images from the Archives of the Institute for Esoteric Research
37 Dollar General
42 Elegy for the Body Before It's Released from Grief and into Light
45 Our Holiday Letter
48 And Still We Gather with Infinite Momentum
50 De Soto Park
52 What Follows Is a Reconstruction Based on the Best Available Evidence
55 HolyMolyLand
57 Peregrinus
61 No Matter How Many Skies Have Fallen
63 Factography: Hometown
64 The Clock of the Long Now
66 Loss Prevention Starts with You
69 But My Heart Is Wild and My Bones Are Steel
70 Post-Game-Day Blessing
73 Vicissitudes
75 Your Rivers, Your Margins, Your Diminutive Villages
77 Poem with Warehouse Fire & Disaster Recovery Team
79 *Too strong*
82 Insane Flying Machines
85 Threat Assessment
92 Jackhammering Limestone
94 I'll Remember You as You Were, Not as What You'll Become

97 *Notes*
99 *Acknowledgments*
102 *About the Author*
108 *Colophon*

ὣς ἄρα φωνήσας πόρε φάρμακον ἀργεϊφόντης
ἐκ γαίης ἐρύσας, καί μοι φύσιν αὐτοῦ ἔδειξε.
ῥίζῃ μὲν μέλαν ἔσκε, γάλακτι δὲ εἴκελον ἄνθος:
μῶλυ δέ μιν καλέουσι θεοί: χαλεπὸν δέ τ᾽ ὀρύσσειν
ἀνδράσι γε θνητοῖσι, θεοὶ δέ τε πάντα δύνανται.

• • •

He pulled the magic plant from the ground.
Its root was black, and its flower was white
as milk. The gods call it moly. Mortals cannot
uproot it, but the gods can do whatever they like.

—*The Odyssey*, Book X (l. 302–306)

HolyMolyLand

In *The Odyssey* there's mention of a plant called moly, which is sacred and harvested only by the gods.

The gods are vengeful but they are also good to us, though we have given up sacrifices and burnt offerings.

With regard to burnt offerings, the following is a concise statement of the Levitical law: these were wholly animal, and the victims were wholly consumed.

The Animal Gang was a marauding group of hooligans who used potatoes studded with razor blades during pitched battles on the streets of Dublin in the 1930s.

Which is to say that the moley was an ordinary potato, its surface jagged with metal edges.

"Holy moley!" was Captain Marvel's characteristic exclamation of surprise.

Because the oath might have been offensive to some, "Holy Moly" was used in the late 1920s as a jocular euphemism for "Holy Moses."

Holy Moses is also a German thrash metal band, known for its lead singer Sabina Classen—one of the first and only women to use a death growl.

Moses demanded the release of the Israelites from slavery, and led them out of Egypt and across the Red Sea. After 40 years of wandering in the desert, he died within sight of the promised land.

In *A Dictionary of the Underworld*, 'moley' is preceeded by 'mokker'—Yiddish for maker.

'Mokker' is a variation of 'macher,' which also means someone who arranges, fixes, or has connections. The person who could miraculously produce a visa or get an exit permit for a Jew was known as a 'macher.'

The story in *The Guardian* of an Austrian Jewish shepherd who drives Syrian refugees across southern Hungary to eastern Austria, hidden under blankets in his car—*All my shoes got torn to pieces at the Hungaaaaaarian border*, he sings, to the tune of a Jewish wedding song, to cheer everyone in his vehicle up.

In *Survival in Auschwitz*, Primo Levi writes, "Perhaps 400 yards from the camp lay the potatoes—a treasure. Two extremely long ditches, full of potatoes and covered by alternate layers of soil and straw to protect them from the cold. Nobody would die of hunger any more."

Concerning the unblemished animals from the herd or the flock: the fire which consumed the offerings was never allowed to go out. Every morning the ashes were conveyed by the priest to a clean place outside the camp.

Many boys in the Animal Gang worked as newspaper vendors—a line of employment that would have given them an intimate awareness of the city and its machinations.

In order to transform into Captain Marvel, homeless newsboy Billy Batson spoke the wizard Shazam's name—an acronym for the wisdom of Solomon, the strength of Hercules, the stamina of Atlas, the power of Zeus, the courage of Achilles, and the speed of Mercury. Speaking the word produced a bolt of magic lightning which transformed Billy into Captain Marvel. Speaking the word again reversed the transformation with another bolt of lightning. This is the way some people believe prayer works.

We are frightened by everything, says one of the Syrian refugees, sitting in the darkness. *Please can we just keep driving.*

"Border Song" is a gospel ballad first performed by Elton John, with lyrics written by Bernie Taupin—except for the final verse, which John wrote himself: *Holy Moses let us live in peace / Let us strive to find a way to make all hatred cease.*

Captain Marvel battled many villains, including Adolf Hitler's champion, Captain Nazi, who was part of the Monster Society of Evil. The Society tried many plans, such as attempting to use Captain Nazi to steal magic fortune-telling pearls, using a film to intimidate the world, and even trying to use a giant cannon to blow holes in countries.

There are holes in all of these stories—open-mouthed gaps in the fence, a singing presence. Holy moly, *please can we just keep driving.*

The phrase "Holy Moley" might have also come from political jingles referencing Professor Raymond Charles Moley, an American economist, and an ally of President Franklin Roosevelt. He served as part of Roosevelt's Brain Trust until he turned against the New Deal and became a conservative Republican.

Our entire country's collective genesis: those who were persecuted, who survived, who fled. My mother was stateless until she was six. She still remembers the rocking of the boat. The *General Harry Taylor*, a converted American troop ship, carried post-war refugees—carried my family—from German displaced persons camps to America in 1952.

Conservative Republicans are generally split on how to handle the Syrian refugee crisis. Senator Ted Cruz (R-Texas) indicated he's against the idea of taking in refugees, saying there are logistical and other challenges. Senator Marco Rubio (R-Florida) has said he's open to the idea of accepting more refugees, as long as security is a top consideration.

Moley wrote the majority of Roosevelt's first inaugural address, but he is not credited with penning the famous line, "the only thing we have to fear is fear itself," though he did write, "only a foolish optimist can deny the dark realities of the moment."

Holy Moses has released the following classic thrash metal albums: *World Chaos*, *Terminal Terror*, *Too Drunk to Fuck*, *Master of Disaster*, *Disorder of the Order*, and *Agony of Death*.

Holy holy holy is the Lord of Hosts. Holy holy holy is the Lord on High.

In 1947 Eleanor Roosevelt visited the DP camp at Bergen-Belsen. The story goes that my grandmother, in the crowd, held my mother up high in the air because she wanted Eleanor to see her red-headed child, born from the ashes.

And in his speech celebrating the 70th anniversary of the liberation of Bergen-Belsen, Ronald Lauder, a big macher in the World Jewish Congress said, *When they begged for help, all they got was silence.* And when he said, *from the ashes of this terrible place*, he meant the large swath of land known as the Field of Ashes, which stretches behind the gas chambers.

And the priest shall take off his linen garments, and put on other garments, and carry forth the ashes outside the camp unto a clean place.

When a reporter interviewed Aphrodite Vati Mariola, whose family owns the Aphrodite Hotel in Lesbos, about the boats of refugees washing up on the beach, she said: *One boy yesterday, he had with him the Bible written in Arabic. It was from a friend of his and he said he was taking care of it. He just kept crying, bursting into tears. And we kept saying, are you OK? And he said no, no, no—I'm OK, I'm just thanking God that I'm alive.*

In 1933, when Franklin Roosevelt was sworn in, he wore a morning coat and striped trousers for the inauguration, and took the oath with his hand on his family Bible, open to I Corinthians 13.

Holy Moly, if I have the gift of prophecy and can fathom all mysteries and all knowledge, and if I have a faith that can move mountains, but do not have love, I am nothing.

There are things I will never know. There are stories that are past telling.

No matter how much testimony we gather. No matter how many details we proclaim.

The space between the hole and the holy, the torn passports, desperation and possibility, the exclamation, the slow vanishing of everything including memory.

AUSTERITY

Go off the fiscal cliff with me, baby. I'm ready.
We can hold hands while we blow through

West Virginia quickly, since we're halfway down
77 past Charleston already, and I'm cranked on

Cherry Coke from Burger King, feet on the dash,
wondering aloud if they'll cart sad Dick Clark out

again for TV New Year's Eve while the car radio
plays Blue Öyster Cult (*I'm burnin' for you*), then

world news: Putin says no Russian adoptions
to the US and you say Dick Clark's a year gone

(heart attack) and the radio says a victim of
gang rape died in India, and that frenzied buyers,

fearful of a ban, are swarming gun stores after
Newtown to stock up on rounds of .223 bullets.

Home in the darkness. Home on the highway. Assault rifles
are sold out across the country. Across the country

we pass trailer parks along the river, empty parking lots
of long-shuttered store fronts, trees hobbled with ice,

and signs left over from Christmas: Happy Birthday
Jesus and Mary Wrapped the Greatest Gift of All.

Congressional leaders are hopeful about a deal, but
I am not confident that anything will change this stretch

of desolate road, this altitudinous mountain we climb
in our four-wheel drive vehicle. Most days it seems

we all might steer directly, without detours, into the white
and constant border. If you ask me if I'm anticipative,

I might say yes. West Virginia, you were Wild and
Wonderful, then Open for Business, but now you're

Wild and Wonderful again because everything comes back,
even Dick Clark, with impaired speech, Beech-Nut gum

sponsorship long gone, to wish us a Happy New Year,
though now it's followed by "Seacrest—out!"

With his perfect teeth and hair, Ryan ushers in
the year of austerity, the year when there was only

evening and morning, the bare trees,
their dark bodies, their bent limbs.

Medium / Message

The rains came last night around sunset,
after a day of grill-heat, a day of persistent

Code Orange air-quality warnings.
Here, there is always a rainbow.

It is slightly biblical, like the yellow bus
that comes every morning to take my son.

I assume he arrives at school, a building
with no interior walls. *Mama, can you come*

make a giant skyscraper? he asks
while I'm writing this. He has inserted

our cat into his family tree, though the teacher
said she doesn't belong there. Or he says

she said that. He is not a reliable witness.
My cousin posts a story on Facebook

as a status: *Yet another neighbor's dog*
started barking excitedly at me and the family

as we strolled down the street. But this time
the dog had a seizure mid-bark and died.

I have nothing profound to say
about pets. I have very little to tell you,

except that everyone is not finally asleep.
They are bracing themselves for the start.

We've been watching the Olympics,
and the crickets and rains have been violent,

but look at that face: completely placid,
completely relaxed. The announcer

is speaking about the runners. There is a bell.
One falls, has fallen on the final lap.

Someone moves to take over the lead.
The man with no legs is running as anchor.

His face is like the sun, and his legs
are pillars of fire. Another man

who had been shot in both legs runs
the start of the relay for our country.

He has to keep the baton from falling
to the ground. We are on our third rainbow

this week. *And when I saw it, I fell on my face,
and I heard the voice of one speaking*, said Ezekiel,

who witnessed the fulfillment of his prophecies.
The single most important factor contributing

to wrongful conviction is eyewitness
misidentification, which is to say that

I think I hear my son calling, wakeful, but
it's only the whine of the air conditioning system,

mechanical, almost human. Everyone
is up tonight to watch a rover land on Mars,

while upstairs, the Lego skyscraper project
is in progress. A sign of the covenant it's not,

but if there is a major event, Legos will survive it.
My son is the cleanup crew in a shaky empire.

Somebody's got to do it, he says, then picks up
a small hammer. Before we know it,

the entire building is gone.

Continuation

And the neighbor's daughter shows my son
the way her father let her hold his gun,

with bullets in it. She was on Adderall,
and now Ritalin, and they're only in

kindergarten but my son doesn't much
like her—the way she brags and lies

and tries to destroy the plants or bugs
around our house, which is the bus stop,

so we head out each morning in our
pajamas, clutching coffee mugs, to wait.

The engine of the bus is huffing,
unmistakable, and we can all hear it

before its yellow nose comes around
the bend. The kids climb the high steps

like they're scaling a great peak.
I can see my son fling his body

into a seat; he waves from the window
while Sarah makes her way to her

mandated spot behind the driver,
who waves to us too, then pulls the lever

to shut the doors and heads down Heartwood
Crossing, though the sign says Xing

as the whole name won't fit. This cross-
hatch, this target; X marks the spot

like those yellow and black novelty
signs: Moose Xing, Gator Xing,

Sasquatch Xing. My son loves to watch
the show *Finding Bigfoot*, where

a research team goes to Rhode Island,
Alaska, New York, to investigate

a recent spike in Squatch sightings.
Each episode is exactly the same,

save for the location: they go out
as a team one night to look for Bigfoot,

call for him, and find signs. Next,
they have a town hall meeting

to discuss sightings with residents
who tell stories, which they recreate

using a giant guy named Bobo as a stand-in,
and they always come to the conclusion

that the resident did see a Bigfoot—
that Bigfoot could definitely live in

_____. We live in blank.
Sarah's mother threw her father out

for keeping a loaded Uzi on the floor
of their garage. When Sarah aims,

with her fingers, at the empty birds' nests
in the eaves of our porch, I wait for her

to say bang, but instead she repeats,
It had bullets in it, and there's the bus

wheezing around the bend again,
yellow as a road sign, a daffodil,

a stretch of CAUTION tape.

Hat Trick

We are snowed in again so we watch
Voldemort remove the Elder Wand
from Dumbledore's tomb. How big
my son's feet are when they stretch
past the blanket we are sharing, past
the slice of sunlight casting us in sharper
and sharper light. I am keeping a list
of what I did today. I have showered.
I have stayed in my pajamas. I have
typed on my laptop in the kitchen.
I have bought Girl Scout cookies in
my pajamas from the neighbor-girl,
Isabelle, who rang the doorbell holding
bright boxes of Peanut Butter Patties
and Thin Mints. I do not tell my son
about my mother's constant refrain—
that Girl Scout uniforms reminded
her of Hitler Youth each time we'd
see a folding table of girls in their
tan vests and pinned sashes outside
Pathmark. This is not extreme
given our family history, but I think
other moms on the block who post
memes like, "Technically you're not
drinking alone if your kids are home"
on the neighborhood Facebook group
and sell handbags or weight loss
shake mix in their spare time would
maybe not understand this particular
trigger. Voldemort is shooting green
lightning from his wand again, and
I have seen the frozen white face of

Dumbledore, impassive, as the camera
pans into his white marble tomb,
lingers on his long white beard.
He pried it from his cold, dead hands!
shouts my son, at the screen, as if he's
been waiting to use this exact phrase
for a long time. I have washed escarole.
I have made Italian wedding soup with
tiny meatballs in it. I have wondered
if we will run out of food before the town
plows us out. Snowzilla, Winter Storm Jonas,
or whatever we name this endless stretch
of white. I have sketched a picture of my
son's favorite hat: a blue faux-fur-lined
Russian bomber with ear flaps, which he
refers to as *hashtag hat*. He often
wears it around the house, though
we keep the heat up. I get that.
I have ordered myself a #hat on
Amazon so I can wear it next time
it snows. So I can go out at night
when the whole block is orange-skied
and quiet, and every house muffles itself
from the street; their windows become
faces I watch and watch. When it falls,
the snow sounds like sugar on foamed
milk, like turning a page in a delicate book.
I haven't told my son the stories about
my grandparents—the ill-fitting wooden
clogs all the prisoners wore through
the winter and stuffed with rags for the
long walk from the camps to the factory
and back in the snow. When my grandfather
came to America he made sweatshop hats,
then opened a factory and copied popular

styles from movies: Barbra Streisand's
leopard print fake fur number in *Funny Girl*,
her plaid newsboy cap from *What's Up, Doc?*
He was not a milliner, but he taught me
to sew, pressed puffed fabric down into
a neat seam with his long pinky nail
while his machine spit out fake mink
pillboxes or folded Cossacks people
wore to navigate the winter streets of
Manhattan. Our neighborhood is
whited out. *Hello gorgeous,* says Barbra.

Double Sonnet Ending in New Testament

This poem is meant to have the make & model
of a vehicle in it, include a food I dislike, a musical
instrument. He gave up the cello. There were multiple
mandolins on his worktable. An item that is broken
beyond repair? My body. That's easy. This & this
& this. A love note that falls into the wrong hands?
Every poem I have ever written. Please stop posting
your thumbs-up sonogram pictures. I don't care
if you're 43. If you're an exception or a miracle or
whatever you are. A bird of prey. His son was learning
to be a falconer. Are these like vultures? I'm not sure.
An item of lost clothing—this doesn't happen often
now that I'm married. Remember those bras
that went missing in apartments, knapsacks, cars?

Bless that time: fear of conception. Holy ruckery
& whiskey & some guy. I drive the highway
in my Honda Civic to the phlebotomist, try to arrive
early to avoid the trainee who always leaves
the bloodless needle halfway in my arm, then
calls for help to the other woman who looks like
a former heroin addict or the Mennonite; both can
deftly navigate my scarred veins. Falcons are
the fastest moving creatures on earth. Your baby
this week is the size of a poppy seed, a sweet pea,
a black olive. I hate olives. In the lab, they play
Spirit FM & don't know anything about me. The DJ
croons, "I am the vine & you are the branches. Those
who remain in me, & I in them, will bear much fruit."

On the Road

We are trying to get pregnant
so everything makes me weep:

the amorphous metal sculpture
shaped like a tree on fire

outside the regional airport.
A young woman with prosthetic

legs standing in baggage claim.
And at the gate in Detroit, a father

stroking his daughter's hair while she
sleeps, head in his lap. My motel

is in a strip mall, next to Lowe's
Home Improvement, and when I walk

out into the world, into the acres
of parking lot which reek of fertilizer

and blacktop, I am ashamed of my own
impatience, which drives me to CVS

for a First Response Rapid Result
pregnancy test stick, which will pink up

to one line or two. Next, the Denny's,
where a pair of day laborers in from

Mississippi drink sweet tea at the counter,
tell the waitress they renovate houses,

ask where folks go to party around here.
They both have home-done tattoos; the one

with Thug Life on the side of his calf
lost all his money riverboat gambling,

says, *Didyouhear about that nineteen-
year-old kid who jumped from the top*

of that floating casino? The men
came in together but sit a few stools

apart, and both look when a petite blonde
runs in late muttering about her class

going till 6, pulls her apron over her head,
calls the brunette *Pickles,* which momentarily

wrenches the melancholy from my body.
Pickles. I am waiting. I am waiting

for my salad-to-go. I will walk back
across the strip mall parking lot,

CVS bag tucked into my purse,
past one blue shopping cart, knocked

over, joy-ridden. There is no part
of the reproduction process that is not

fraught, and as soon as the automatic
motel doors part, I will feel stabbing

cramps, get my period in the elevator up.
In my room, beyond the blackout curtains

lighted signs on sticks raise their hands
in the dusk: Marathon, Schnucks,

McDonald's golden arches tenting
the night with overwhelming sadness.

There are questions no one can answer
for me, no matter how long

I wait patiently. O vacant space.
O single-lined body of flesh and blood.

Diaspora

I am riding the F train to Brooklyn
with my son, who is Appalachian
as much as anything, who is six and
does not notice the Hasidic women
reading Tehilim on their way home,
praying psalms from worn leather-
bound siddurim, moving their lips
past Broadway, Second Avenue,
Delancey, and he would not know
to identify them by their below-
the-knee skirts, the filled in parts
of their sheitels where scalp should
be visible, or the Brighton Beach men
in gray fedoras with threatening hand
tattoos speaking Russian, the occasional
wondrous mosaic murals or regular
green and white tiles spelling station
names: Bergen St., Carroll St., Smith
9th St., my son discovering he can see
his own reflection in the windows
of the cars when they plunge into
dark tunnels while the women's lips
keep moving, and I want to tell him
I know their kind, though I know
to say this is reductive or offensive,
even if I might say it too about the
bleach blond with the septum ring,
or the old Russian mobsters, so
when he says, *It's hard to believe that
you got off here everyday*, I agree and
think of all the times I climbed
the station stairs or felt the give

of metal turnstiles on my hips,
the jangle of apartment keys or
click of my own heels on pavement
after a night out too late, the car service
guys playing dominoes on overturned
crates outside the bodega who didn't
look up, and the way the trains still
vibrate beneath the surface with exactly
the same frequency they always did,
blowing hot air through the grates,
rattling me to the bone with foreboding
joy, and I want to tell him I know this
exact moment, the one where you finally
learn the contours of your own face,
its beauty as it hurtles through darkness.

Images from the Archives of the Institute for Esoteric Research

Some days the whole neighborhood is shrouded
in a secret language or gesture, small collisions,
like our wind chimes, which never stop

hounding each other, like the neighbor
who drove to see his dead mother but
he got there and she wasn't dead—as it

turns out there was nothing scientific
about his trip to Florida—as it turns out
an egg floats in glass somewhere

due to maybe saline, maybe wire,
while a metal arm conducts measurements
of how high the egg, how diminished the water.

There is space between what we see
and the actual, which means there is no such thing
as absolute proof, only competing accounts

of causality & truth & home and there is death
(always death) and a shared burial committee
here. Since we live in a small town

we are our own and only community: behold
our dark and magnificent horror, our holy
fellowship of caretakers, our rotating attendants

who sit by a body all night reciting psalms:
blessed   why   help   I am desolate and afflicted;
we watch and watch and watch and then

ask the deceased for forgiveness since ~~we fell~~
~~asleep and our dreams were sweet~~ we are all held
by invisible wire, and in those moments we are delicate

scales filled with thumbtacks (face up) and hair.
Let me tell you about the nest in our eaves:
one bird left and another moved in so

every time we opened the front door
that new bird flew out towards the mountains
in a straight line. Feathers still litter our walkway,

and someone stuffs them into a test tube
mounted on a pedestal with clamps. That person
is doing research on the domestic.

They are doing an investigation on home.
An egg is cradled in a sling. It shines white
like a moon. Maybe it is mine. Or maybe

there is rope connecting two glasses,
one propped on a set of books no one will ever read
no matter how lonely they are. How lonely are you?

Would you resurrect an extinct animal, since it's now
biologically possible (genome sequencing) like the scientists
who plan to grow a mammoth (in the womb of an elephant)

cloned from one found frozen in the Siberian tundra
(the white and constant border) so long ago in a time
before unfamiliar speech I did not understand

there are different paths to resurrection (kind of
a neat trick) though the melancholy will inhabit
our bodies until the holy spirit becomes

plausible (I am desolate and afflicted though
we are faithful and scientific) and
this explanation (incontrovertible) for an empty

A-frame, a fiction, the wind chimes snapped
the neighbor evacuated the approaching storm
means I dwell among you and you and you.

DOLLAR GENERAL

At the Dollar General before Christmas
a woman muttering to herself in Gift Wrap

picks out a roll of pastel paper that's clearly meant
for a baby shower—ducks, bottles, lavender

safety pins—then asks me if I think it's all right
for a baby shower. I tell her it's cute, and

when she holds up two enormous cotton candy
pink gift bows, and asks me to choose, I point

to the one with small pink feet dangling in plastic
from the bow's center, which looks cheaper

than the plainer option, but more festive,
and who doesn't like festive? Everyone in town

is buying stocking stuffers, and in the next aisle,
a familiar woman juggling bubble bath and pencils

waves hello—I only know her as Kate's mom—
and she's actually wearing one of those

floor-length green and red wool plaid skirts
featured exclusively in holiday catalogs with

faux family photo spreads of tree-trimming
parties. Near a pyramid of cookie tins,

there's a kindergarten teacher I also recognize
from my son's school, out with her teenage son,

loading up on frozen pizzas and Sunbeam bread.
What are the details I've left out? That I'm not

poor. That I've never had to buy food
at the Dollar Store at the end of the month.

That I've been relentlessly straightforward lately,
which has to do with my need to explain

exactly what happened, because what happened
is so unclear. There is never enough information

about my neighbors, about the ways in which
people live. I've been living in the South now

for most of my adult life. You shall love your
neighbor as yourself, says Leviticus 19:18,

and the Hebrew word for neighbor is *ray'ah,*
meaning *friend, companion, fellow, other.* I am

neighbor and other. I am a Jew and the mother
of one white son and one black son. I've been

writing about guns lately, but this is not really
a poem about guns—it's about Christmas, though

some people think I've declared war on the holiday
when I wish them *Happy Holidays* instead of *Merry*

Christmas. We are the only Jewish family in the
neighborhood, which isn't a problem, except

around holiday time, when I'm sure our house
is the saddest on the block because it is unlit.

When we had lunch to chat about adoption,
my neighbor—my neighbor who is also

infertile—my neighbor, whom I do not see
in Dollar General—my neighbor, who has three

Christmas trees in her house and garland wrapped
on every handrail and mantel—she asks me about

the home study process: when a social worker
comes to your house to assess how you live,

what kind of family you are, whether you have
fire extinguishers on each floor and keep your

firearms locked up. *Make sure your firearms
are locked up,* our social worker would say

on the phone before each visit, and I'd remind her
that we own no guns. *What kind of people own guns?*

I'd think as I hung up the phone. My neighbor
and I share a plate of onion rings and become

teary over our intimate infertility heartbreak.
She says, *Good thing I got John a new*

gun safe for Christmas. On clear days, when
I walk the roads, sometimes with my neighbors,

I hear people shooting off their weapons
at the firing range in the distance. Which is

to say it's not surprising that in the past year
there have been over thirty thousand gun

deaths in the United States. Which is to say
there are many people I have compassion for,

like the woman in the Gift Wrap aisle who maybe
had some kind of slight disability. And there are

many things that make me furious, like the fact
that we pay our schoolteachers so little

they have to shop for groceries at Dollar General
at the end of the month because smaller quantities

cost less. My son's first grade teacher runs
a family side business called Ruttin' Camo &

Grafix where she and her husband sell
Redneck Stemware in camouflage patterns

made from mason jars, and also custom hydro-
dipped firearms. In their Etsy "About" section

they say they are a small family-owned business.
They say they started putting hydrographics

on mason jars on a whim, to help pay for expenses
at gun shows. At gun shows in Virginia, you can

still purchase a gun, a high-capacity magazine,
an assault weapon with no background check

or waiting period. You need only be eighteen and
bring two forms of ID. You can walk off with your

purchase. We've seen my son's first grade teacher
working her family booth at craft fairs, at the Pumpkin

Patch next to the Kettle Corn folks. I always
make him go over to her and say hello.

She is quite strict so he doesn't always want to,
but I push him toward the camo'd mason jars

on their leggy stems. *Say hello to Mrs. Giles,*
I say, and he does. What are the details

I've left out? That this year I asked my husband
to hang icicle lights from the eaves.

That each night before bed, one of us opens
the front door, unplugs the extension cord,

and the house goes dark.

Elegy for the Body Before It's Released from Grief and into Light

I. Pallbearers, St. Ann, Communion of Saints Parish (Cleveland, OH)

I take a surreptitious photo of the grandsons—
eight of them, which isn't even all of them—
bearing her gunmetal casket up the stairs
of St. Ann in dark suits, bowing their heads
into the driving snow. Ann was the mother
of Mary, grandmother of Jesus Christ. She is
the patron saint of Detroit, miners, mothers,
and moving house. She is the patron saint of

carpenters, poverty, pregnancy, the childless,
and sterility. These men—they're no longer boys,
many are over forty—carry their grandmother
slow, ceremoniously, level with their hips,
arms straight. Watch them, their sheer numbers,
their black dress shoes shuffling forward over
salt and stone. Ann was barren until Joachim
went into the desert to plead with God.

Until Ann cried out to the Lord, *Why
was I born?* St. Ann's emblem is a door.
The chapel is open and blazingly white.
We enter behind the coffin, now on wheels,
draped in bone-colored cloth. I can tell you
about the houses of Detroit, vacant and
falling in on themselves. I can tell you
about the scar in the crook of my elbow

from the phlebotomist's needle over
and over. I can tell you about the frescoes
flanking the altar: an ascended Mary
standing on a crescent moon, buoyed
by a pile of winged cherubim, or Joseph
cradling baby Jesus alongside a flowering staff
of lilies. I can tell you what it's like to carry
only one body into this world: the slow weight,
the scalpel and the sheet.

II. Haec Est Domus Dei

You've heard this story already, but it bears
repeating: Ann and Joachim were childless
until grief drove Joachim into the wilderness,

until Ann wept in a garden, under a laurel.
*I am not like this earth because even the earth
brings forth its fruit.* This is the point

where angels appear, but no angels appeared
to us, and no baby, even after the trips
to fertility clinics across four states, the plastic

jugs of needles, the hormones, the bargaining
with God. Maybe I had nothing to offer.
Maybe I didn't promise enough, weep

enough, open my palms wide enough
in supplication. When I joined
the legions of women who asked God

to open their wombs, be made abundant,
I was silent, thought *fist of light* and *come
into my heart you motherfucker.* If I could

do it over again, I wouldn't ask for a
child, but say Lord, with your bonds
of perfection, wrench this melancholy

from my body, this container, this ship
called grief that's failed to deliver
what we've asked of it. My suitcase

of impatience. My mask of sadness.
It is not our duty to praise these things
heaped upon us since I am a body

of flesh and blood, arms outstretched, palms
turned up, fists clenched and unclenched
to assist the phlebotomist, angel of mercy,

in filling her vials. Bless the sweet
dumbness of a body heavy with longing—
the body in its damaged, flooded, shining

state. Its mute surface. Bless the places
where there is no light, and the aftermath:
I am not my body. But I am.

OUR HOLIDAY LETTER

Our holiday letter
is covered in flocked velvet
and bitterness. It starts

with dear friends. We've had
a hard year. I write this
while coughing. I write this

in a place of not-knowing
(despite the season)
if we are healthy, or safe,

or long-lasting. My son
comes home and complains
about Christmas in school—

the songs Ruby's dad
played on his guitar,
the songs they sang

with Mrs. Quesenberry
in Assembly. He could not
name any of the songs.

On the bus, he told Brady
that Santa doesn't exist
and Brady's mother

sent me an angry
text about childhood,
about wanting her son

to remain blissful longer
and I wasn't sure what
to write back. Dear

friends. This year
has dragged like
a broken tailpipe,

all scrapes and sparks,
but I'm telling you,
though we've been

tested and tested,
most days, we still
feel blessed, and

wish you peace
in spite of our
hardships, and

maybe joy,
though yesterday
twenty children

were gunned down
in an elementary
school, and is there

anyone who isn't
thinking about
every same weekday

morning—we wave
to the dark squares
of yellow bus windows

our only child rides
to a place where they
sing songs he's never

heard. *What were
some of the words?*
I ask him, and he

can't answer. Dear
friends. Our holiday
letter this year will

be brief. There's been
illness and tragedy,
disappointment and some

anguish. We've kicked
this year down the hill
like a half-deflated,

stuttering soccer ball.
But now there are
children forming delicate

chains with their arms
on each other's
shoulders—children

being led to safety.
There are children
here. Dear friends.

And Still We Gather with Infinite Momentum

The Promised LAN is the name
of a wireless network that pops up
on my phone as we drive 250 near
Wooster in flurries, in almost-dark,

while cops wave us past with
lighted batons that signal incident,
that motion please-look-at-this-
catastrophe. And there it is,

framed by silent fire trucks
banked on the side of the road:
a candy apple red car flipped
in a ditch and crushed,

roof flattened, windows
blown out. The lights
of emergency vehicles
flash yellow, blue, white,

make the night dangerously
festive, give the surrounding
houses, with their inflatables
and LED icicles, their luminaries

and their radiant nativity sets
a run for their money. The men
with neon flares windmill
their glowing arms to assure us

we are all under the care
of strangers—earlier, the IHOP

waitress with the whiskey voice
named Mary who told us

we brought the sunshine,
then the hostesses dressed
as elves smoking in the parking lot
of the next-door Pilot, flirting

with truckers. Was it an Amish
buggy that distracted the driver
of that car? Deer prancing
across the asphalt at dusk?

It is almost Christmas
and everyone is in on the act,
even the radio, even this accident.
On an overpass nearby in red

spray paint: I LOVE YOU BABYDOLL.
We love you babydoll. We love you
person on a gurney. Get well soon.
We drive past your wreckage

without stopping while everyone's
signals cross: default, linksys, virus,
GodisGreat, youfoundme, getlost,
JEMguest, batcave, funkchance.

De Soto Park

"What if the moon was essence of quinine"
—Frank Stanford

everyday antidote for numerous maladies my grandmother drank
tonic water in yellow bottles—something to do with her restless legs

at night or was it the morning in Florida maybe after the Early Bird Special
which was actually afternoon with that blistering sun on the Boulevard

along the ocean & then the Intracoastal where signs warned boat propellers
from manatee since some creature was near extinction, some creature bled—

or was it something to do with the girls who had Russian soldiers chasing
after them, since it was always someone during the war or after but no one

mentioned the war exactly: a story without an end in which they all came to America
to play cards & raise children—my grandmother, you should have seen her

at poker in her turban, North Miami so hot anytime including December
but no one minded—not the grandparents, not the children, not the grandchildren

since the humidity was our country: the humidity & the night-swimming,
our slick adolescent bodies like dolphins until golf-cart security chased us out,

though the condo pool was lit—even when it was shuttered & locked—
with underwater domes that pockmarked the surface like luminary moons

even when nothing shined down on the Atlantic up the block where we escaped
to dodge man-o-wars on the beach & shiver exquisitely in each other's dark arms

then hopped chain-link fences or tore across metal drawbridges past midnight
to florescent elevator banks with someone else's grandmother yelling:

I thought you were dead, I thought you were in a ditch, but it wasn't a ditch:
we were drunk on strangers who were not strangers: we were the same tribe

of survivors, a dream country everyday in this state of ocean & oranges & tattooed
Yiddish grandparents—so what if at night we were restless and overly-loved

& only the sounds of chairs scraping linoleum waiting up: a tissue, a wheelbarrow,
the shovels, the camps, the cards, my grandmother asking if I wanted something

to eat & there I was always saying *yes*—there's no choice—because in this place
no one is really in danger & no one ever gets full

What Follows Is a Reconstruction Based on the Best Available Evidence

we went to the aquarium
each year and pressed
our palms to the tank-fronts

the halls were enveloped
in dusk and everything else
was lit from within

bioluminescence is relevant
to the fact that on television
all we need to leave behind

is the smallest smudge
to be identified positively
in an electronic database

sunrise over the bridge
and a siren in the opening
credits always a siren in the

distance a child selects
a nose a hat a silhouette
on screen to make a likeness

for some crimes
we can ask forgiveness
but for others only

silence   a blank   the sound
of radio static in place of
an emergency broadcast

who or what will instruct
us nights when we sleep
under orange skies with

go bags potable liquids
power bars passports first-
aid kits batteries agility the

scaffolding of fear and
bone covered in tender skin
and pray morning is mortal

again when we wonder
where startled creatures
hide in large storms

when the aquarium tanks
fill with brackish water quickly
and fish have gone missing

and proud roller coasters
are swept under—when
whole neighborhoods

smolder from embers
carried on the wind
that fix under shingles

we are burning we are
lashed to the mast of a ship
speeding past an entire

city calling danger, neon,
desire, calling us in its
shining wrecked voice

of latent catastrophe
when sailors reported
seeing mermaids or sirens

they were probably
seeing dugongs or
manatee instead

something from the order
of sirenians, a species,
a classification, this group

moves gentle, glacial even,
can be harmed I know it now—
we can all be harmed

HolyMolyLand

is a place we all pass through (of violence, of revelation) with grand opening
    flags strung above fenced-in lots & railroad crossings.

Holy is the _____ _____ almighty.

And we inscribe the darkest days of history on our own bodies, sometimes
    invisibly—the way skateboarders carve asphalt & metal—& sometimes we
    open our shirts and say look

at this door caught in a hail of bullets, pockmarked; my heart

beats a tattoo in my chest: a knocking rat-tat-tat; the body is impenetrable,
    save through desire or violence. So it came to pass

that over the decades, some survivors played their faded numbers in the
    lottery or used them as passwords. & this

is our encrypted language ~~of suffering,~~ of protection. We are surrounded by an
    emptiness filled with signs.

I ask my son what he would do if someone came to his school with a gun.
I would take my friends & hide, he says. *I would be very quiet.*

My son, whom I carried that long summer, through the chalked & blood-
    soaked streets of Southeast tucked into my body.

My body: burnt-edged chipboard construction, Tyvek paper torn & flapping
    in the wind against a plywood frame stamped with a manufacturer's
    imprint.

The security guards ask us to remove everything from our pockets—even lint.

& here is the officer who says, *God creates the forgetfulness so we can forget.*

Holy is _____'s name.

& here is the Secret Annex, the movable bookcase that served as the door &
   entrance to the family's hiding place. My innards:

tufted insulating foam cut into shapes of billboards, highway overpasses, fast
   food marquees—a dense pink thicket held together with roofing nails &
   pylons.

& here are the sounds of the shooting range up the road: a series of echoes
   that sweep the dust, tilt the evergreens slightly

into silence-blank-silence-blank, then air—for a moment before the crack of
   the board's wheels hitting pavement again. Another body

in motion, a vulnerable flesh. Our ubiquitous yet easily overlooked emblems
   of transient existence are heaped one on top of the other, as in a landfill,
   giving the place an air of neglect.

Holy is the _____ of _____.

Peregrinus

i. (one who has come from afar)

There was the time I stayed at that
cruise ship hotel permanently docked
in Rotterdam, where the floor of my cabin
at the ship's prow sloped up like a ramp,
as if I were about to launch myself into the
North Sea. Mornings, we were socked in
by fog thick as a gray wool scarf.
The other passengers all seemed to be
Dutch so I sat by a window drinking coffee
in silence, looking out into the furred distance
lined with stacked shipping containers.

ii. (who is on a journey to a holy place)

In the 16th century, pilgrims on wanderings
were identified by fixed attributes:
the staff, the shoulder bag, the badges
on their broad-brimmed hats. I am not
a wanderer, but I ride on a lot of airplanes.
I do not usually recline my seat.
The aisle makes me feel less claustrophobic.
When I drive home from the airport
over the mountains in the evening there's
fog again through headlights, more like gauze,
as if the entire town has been bandaged.
When I return home, I often think *estuary*
or *why aren't the curtains closed since
it's night?* When I return this time,
the pumpkins have collapsed in on themselves

on the porch and it's raining. Like any
passing stranger, I can see clearly
into my own lit house.

III. (A PHYSICAL JOURNEY—OFTEN ON FOOT)

The ways in which this town has been rent
apart are too numerous to list, but I will
try anyway: the largest mass shooting at
a university, the beheading in the Au Bon Pain,
the Caldwell Fields murders still unsolved,
an execution of a campus officer in his cruiser,
the student found dead in the trunk of another
student's car, the local teen girl whose throat
was slashed by two more students, and then
the regular threats—this week, *Death to Muslims*
scrawled in a bathroom stall in the student center.

IV. (DEFINED AS A PERIOD OF EXILE)

When Maria Loopuyt left home in 1936
because her father was against her marriage
to an architect, she went to stay with painter
Carel Willink. One day Willink said to her,
*Put on a beautiful dress and I will make
a portrait of you,* and he did. I saw it hanging
in the Museum Boijmans Van Beuningen
where there was also an unfinished wooden table
with a green neon sign resting on it that said
Leave a Piece of Yourself Behind. The table
was covered in business cards, gum, used tickets,
change of many currencies, the inconsequential
pocket detritus of hundreds of visitors.

V. (THE EXPERIENCE OF LIFE IN THE WORLD)

I thought about leaving a waterlogged
wallet photo of my oldest son, wrinkled,
faded, but was sure it had become a talisman
from living so long in my wallet that certain
tragedy would befall me if I removed it,
even if I sent him to Rotterdam one day
to look for himself. In another picture
in the museum, a peasant dances the egg dance
at an inn. We do not know exactly how
the dance was performed, but the egg
had to be left intact. *Put on a beautiful dress,*
and I will make a portrait of you, I said
to the town.

VI. (FROM A STATE OF WRETCHEDNESS TO A STATE OF BEATITUDE)

There were women in hijab on every metro
platform in Rotterdam: Stadhuis, Beurs, Rijnhaven.
They belonged as much as anyone, which means
they were mostly imperceptible due to numbers.
Or at least not singular. They were from (t)here.
Some accounts of the egg dance say it had to be
performed blindfolded, or only on one foot,
with hands at your sides. If a young couple
finished the dance without breaking an egg,
they were betrothed, and not even an obdurate
parent could oppose the marriage. The Talmud
(Shabbat 31a) tells of a man who asked the sage Hillel
to teach him the entire Torah while standing
on one foot. *What is hateful to you, do not do*
to your neighbor, said Hillel. *That's it.*
All the rest is commentary. Now go and learn it.

Next to *Landscape with Shipwreck* by Frederik van Valckenborch, a note says, *Every attempt to recognize a specific story in this scene has failed.*

No Matter How Many Skies Have Fallen

Let's say we are making a list,
and it's not about how to be

good or zombie foreclosures
or anything resembling distress

calls from an airline going down
in a cluster of trees. Someone

says, *I've got a situation here,*
but they don't mean that holiday

picture of you dangling handcuffs
from your index finger or the fact

that your mother loved you
very much until we enhanced

the audio. Let's say we are in
violation of the local housing

code, which specifies the number
of outlets per room where we can

plug in to the network that says
Join Other Network or Airport: On.

The overhead compartments groan
under the weight of our collective

sadness and in the emergency exit
row we must speak English, confirm

with a loud yes that we're willing
to perform certain duties. We agree

to rescue each other and strangers
who also glance sideways at street

grids from above during takeoff,
chew gum while we rise past what-

ever their threshold for fear or
adventure. We are under the care

of each other and sometimes we
fail mightily to contain the damage:

the house picked clean by scavengers,
the hanging gutters, collapsed garage.

FACTOGRAPHY: HOMETOWN

down by the water who can even remember
driving over the bridge at night

or cassette tapes: winding their unraveled
innards with a pencil, this reinsertion

of a familiar, slightly mangled melody—
the men with home-scratched

tattoos fishing the docks, a clear
jellyfish the size of a dime bag

bobbing in a plastic bucket
like a ziplock of organs unmoored—

this moment of transit, of taking
a body, this boundary from which

something begins its presencing

The Clock of the Long Now

I know what's going down out there
from the apocalyptic sunsets lately
scraping the sky red and purple like
a bruised clavicle. It's a tiny minuscule

bit of noise, but still: the litter of fences
and factories, the town seeping like a stain
into the surrounding fields. When Monet
couldn't tolerate the incoherence

of the streets, he went back to painting
landscapes he would construct himself
just for the purpose of painting them.
And I'm telling the truth when I say

I've heard a guy busking on his guitar
in the strip mall outside the Goodwill
and next to the Food Lion. When I go in
for groceries, he's singing, "I have become

comfortably numb," a little high and
a little sharp, and then when I come out,
he's doing "Hallelujah," and both of these
sentiments are simultaneously accurate:

DepressedBlessed would be the hashtag.
On the car radio today a woman lectured
about mid-life, told us to have goals, get
hobbies, create our own milestones

around athletics. I take notes on an
orange and yellow Virginia Lottery

Ticket with a stubby pencil: *mark
boxes as shown* ☒. When my son

ate a pencil—colored, blue—his tongue
became an ocean of sorrow. A group
of sea otters resting together is called
a raft. You and I, we lashed whatever

we had in our pockets with string
and set the parcel gently on the sea.
I've heard the sounds of a waterfall
cascading from 148 speakers. I've

heard the cat crunching kibble and
the trees shushing the fields as I write this.
I've heard the rubber band that binds
us extricably to one another snap back

against our skin and leave a mark.
I've heard a car engine gasp, then
turn over in the parking lot of that
numb hallelujah strip mall and maybe

Monet was onto something. In his
painting *Boulevard Saint-Denis, Argenteuil,
in Winter*, he captures the exact moment
the sun struggles to break through

a light snowfall. There's a path, a fence,
a town, figures hurrying with umbrellas.
Snow takes the edges off of most things,
but the sun—its yellow light riveting,

sickly, the opposite of triumphant.

Loss Prevention Starts with You

The letter that I'm
too frightened to write
would say what?

That the body is only {this}
wanting thing disguised
as a plane landing,

arms alight? My body
is a city, one of many
destinations buckled in

to a seat, upright, and
the letter I try to write
instead limns the misfortune

of others, my hairdresser
indicted in Wythe County
on charges of driving

under the influence
and possession—
third or subsequent

offense, but it seems
better than everyone else's
indictments, which were counts

of having a child present
while making meth. Possession
is nine-tenths of the law

and our bodies remember
their internments, ingest
their sorrows, hold on

to whatever rubs up
against them; *the body
is everything*, I think,

but I don't write that.
Tonight, past the runway,
wind chimes speak

through the mountains.
A fast train hollers after itself.
Where is your body?

Lifting off like this plane
from somewhere dark
and nondescript, hovering

like the pages of newspaper
from a town I don't live in
when my seatmate folds a story

over my tray so I can see
the Clearbrook Walmart
where a man exposed himself

to three girls inside and they're
requesting the public's help
to identify the man stalking

the seasonal aisle in his red-
and-white striped shirt,
his khaki pants. He drives off,

the male subject. And hallelujah,
you should see the traffic
from the air, it looks like

light-loving snakes tenderly
clutching themselves around
rivers and other stumbling blocks.

But My Heart Is Wild and My Bones Are Steel

and there's the bag boy in his hoodie
and yellow safety vest again riding

a silver train of eight shopping carts
stacked into each other shuddering

across the salted asphalt parking lot,
his gloved hands grasping the last

handle as he stands on the bar
over the wheels, leans in and rides

them hard through the automatic
doors of the nearly-empty Food Lion

with some glee or abandon, the clatter
is night-driven, the clatter is no one

can see him except all of us pulling up
past the plastic sheeting that keeps the wreaths

and trees-for-sale from weather it's late
December and snowing the carts nest

within each other to facilitate collection
are able to carry a child though I am not

though twenty four thousand children
are injured each year in shopping carts

and none of us hear a sound except
I want I want I want

POST-GAME-DAY BLESSING

Bless the black G-string,
abandoned on the sidewalk
beside a green ginkgo
sapling on Lee Street.
Bless the girl who
shimmied out of it
before dawn, drunk
on Curaçao or Triple
Sec or Mike's Hard
Lemonade. Drunk
on lust and early autumn
and our team's unexpected
win over Georgia Tech.
Bless our team, all defense,
no offense. Bless every-
one who must have been
downtown last night
with their car flags and
war whoops, mesh jerseys
and micro-minis. Bless
our star quarterback, on fire
with a 14-3 halftime lead.
We are on the first grade
class walking trip to the
library so everyone can
get their own cards. I am
chaperone, which means
herding kids out of traffic,
back over the curb. Bless
the curb, and the kids who
use it as a balance beam.
Bless the magical book drop.

Bless the girl with knotted
hair who tries to stuff orange
leaves into the slot. And
bless the librarian, too, who
reads a book, loudly, clearly,
to everyone about someone
reading a spooky book. Bless
the meta-story, and the mass
of first graders, descending
on the stacks like locusts.
Bless the red solo cups
on the return trip
congregating like plastic
flames, like oversized
maraschino cherries on
the early-morning lawns
of Phi Delt, Sig Ep,
any dilapidated white
house with a porch
couch on East Roanoke
Street. Bless the empty
bottles of PBR knocked
on their sides, mouths
open in wondrous O's.
O rushing yards. O Bud
Light Lime in your crushed
cardboard case resting
on the elementary school
lawn. Bless my son and
his friend Major, who look
past the blue Trojan wrapper
on Jackson Street, the flattened
Miller Lite can on Bennett,
to the blue butterfly,
to the giant mushroom

blooming in the corner
of someone's yard. *It looks*
like a piece of meat, says
my son. *Or a tree stump*,
says Major, matter-of-factly.
It is a mushroom worth
blessing. And bless our team
for escaping Bobby Dodd Stadium
with a 17-10 win. Bless us for
being able to hold on despite
the onslaught.

Vicissitudes

The man who comes to view the mistakes in the yard is a turf expert

I point out the red thread disease overtaking patches of lawn that are withered
and brown

He says different poisons will knock out the poison ivy and silverthorn

I've been bitten by something that itches (the vicissitudes of daily life?)

I wash the accidental pee off blue sandals

I wash the red clay dust from yellow rain boots

Carry me, say the small dead spiders in every ceramic cup, who tuck
themselves, too, between carpet and moldings

The carpool father asks if McDonald's for dinner was okay when he comes to
the door to deliver my older son

And I am grateful for my son stumbling in, batting helmet blue in his hand,
which thunks when he sets it down in the foyer

His small box of leftover McNuggets, his sweaty head, his bat bag slung off
his shoulder

I send him up to the shower

Rabbi Tarfon said it is not your responsibility to finish the work (the dishes in
the sink, the knotted plastic bag from daycare)

He also said you are not free to desist from it

When he said "the work," he meant perfecting the world

My younger son thinks there are ghosts in his room

He says, *Lie down with me* (I don't)

He is stealthy when he drops from his top bunk and appears in the den like a
    ninja

He calls himself *Sister Vampire*

I make him climb the stairs again, and he again asks for water

I tell him if he closes his eyes and stays under the covers, I'll be back to check
    on him (I don't)

There is no one I can depend on to do the work but me

Not the trusty blue whale knick-knack on the mantle

Not the hum of the HVAC or the song of the spring peepers

They are responsible for their own things

The torn paper from the pad on the fridge resting on the counter:
    LOVE YOU ALL! / SEE YOU SOON!

Tomorrow will be June, and I will drag my ennui (or is it sorrow?) into the
    fogless morning

I will sign everyone into school, and try to remember what I was reaching for
    before I lower my hands to my sides and keep walking

Your Rivers, Your Margins, Your Diminutive Villages

We are all as old as each other and the
cashier at Food Lion does not check
my ID for Chardonnay, cards me next time
for the case of PBR, looks at my license

and says, *You're the same age as my mom,*
but you look much younger, and I think
of her hard-living mom—of the women
who come after shift-change at Moog

for bagged salad and Lean Cuisine and
ground beef for the kids and I want to
make it clear that I am at the Food Lion
with my faded tattoos again every day

sometimes more than twice mostly
for my kids since I'm the mom with
the overrun cart and the yelling we've
run out of toilet paper again we're

missing the cheddar or ketchup and
no you can't have that, but today
outside the automatic doors by the
caged propane tanks and water dispenser

and Red Box movies and Coke machine
there's a two-tiered metal stand with hanging
baskets of trailing pansies on the bottom
shadowed by wind chimes with miniature

pastel birdhouses on top and what I want
to tell you is that these stop me: their song

and their otherworldly new age light
speaking at the top of their lungs

trembling against engines revving
and carts shuddering into one another
after groceries are unloaded into trunks
slamming shut—this music the best failure

of my imagination which is usually stuck
on the camo'd pickups or the home piercings
or the plastic bags skittering the curb—
everything other than what it is I think

I am, which is part of this but younger
and ethereal, so what if everywhere had
wind chimes: doctors' waiting rooms
or Jiffy Lube or the DMV? What if

they trailed after us wherever we went
as though our actual steps on concrete
or asphalt or linoleum generated song
that's not quite song but two objects

strung closely together knocked into
each other by randomly generated
breezes—your cart my cart the beverage
aisle: our trembling jittery refrain.

POEM WITH WAREHOUSE FIRE & DISASTER RECOVERY TEAM

"Fire at a Brooklyn Warehouse Puts Private Lives on Display"
—*The New York Times*, 1 February 2015

No lives were lost. Nothing was gutted
but the crumpling warehouse and its contents:
medical forms, court transcripts, sonograms,

bank checks. *They're like treasure maps,*
someone said of the half-charred scraps.
But they weren't. This was the opposite—

it was as if the filing cabinets that compose us
were opened and the detritus of adulthood
poured out and burned to make room again

for vanished loves, childhood pets, snippets
of music and gesture and image and scent—
every piece of ourselves tamped down

by bills and logistics suddenly resurfacing.
Beachcombers picked their way through
remnants half-buried in the sand: a scattering

of records stamped "confidential," and the rest
commonplace, thrown to the wind. Come evening,
the current carried more waves of waterlogged

paper, edges browned, to shore. What appeared
to be a set of chest X-rays landed on a rock—
vulnerable waterfront, how slowly the city opens

the ribcage to its heart. Disaster recovery contractors
in neon jackets and protective boots sealed off
the jetty's entrance with yellow caution tape,

scooped documents from the river with nets.
We're just here to clean up the debris, they said,
and once they started, it was difficult to extinguish

the memories that flared up across the city
in place of depositions, hospital charts, status reports,
W-2s, I-9s, invoices in triplicate. We got it

all back: lilies of the valley. The entirety of
1997 with your hip-bones pressed hard
between my thighs. The stray black cat found

in a window well who lived and lived. An engraved
silver Zippo. The exact slant of pale sun cut
through the one-window walk-up on Atlantic.

The lyrics to "Glory Box," with feedback, with
bass line. The scent of soft roof tar in August.
The name of the bartender at O'Connor's (Spike)

who still did buybacks. Faint brush of lips on neck.
Hallelujah, an arc of spray, like ejaculate, hits
the smoldering metal warehouse husk.

Through a winter haze, broken pilings
rise up from the East River in thanks.

Too strong

is what the announcer dubs Steph Curry's
flubbed shot that bounces diagonally
off the backboard. This is game seven
of the NBA finals, and Cleveland goes on
to defeat the Golden State Warriors,
but we don't know this yet, because
we're still watching the game, jammed
into an alcove where it's live-streaming
from someone's laptop onto a wall at an
artists' colony, since a surprising number
of writers and composers and painters
are basketball fans, so when the sports-
caster reels out descriptions of plays,
Nate the jazz critic says, "Someone should
write a poem called *Too strong*," and
Stephen Dunn isn't interested though
he's sitting behind me also rooting for
the Cavs, saying things like *my goodness*
and *he's the best closer for his size.*
"You have to give context in your poem,"
mansplains Nate, who points out that
'too strong' is a hyper-masculine way
of saying Curry basically just fucked up
the shot. It's important to note here that
Cleveland hasn't won a championship
in any sport since 1964—that's a 52-year
curse in case you're anti-math. I am well-
versed in the sadness of Cleveland—
skies hanging like lead most of the year,
husks of buildings, smokestacks pumping
raw flame over downtown. My husband
grew up in the sadness of Cleveland,

and we return there every Christmas to more
unemployment, more foreclosure, more
poverty, more shitty weather. When LeBron
left Northeast Ohio, my husband actually
burned his replica jersey in the yard, wouldn't
mention his name for three long years of anger
and mourning. He uses Cleveland sports teams
to teach our sons about failure and perseverance,
with a heavy emphasis on the failure. But
here's LeBron on screen, lugging his city's
championship dreams like a bag of rocks.
Forget Tamir Rice, age twelve, gunned down
by police for being black, for playing with
a toy gun in a park, left to bleed out on a
sidewalk. Forget that Cleveland is the
poorest city in America other than Detroit.
LeBron's stuffed this game with thunderous
dunks, fadeaway jumpers, and blocked shots,
towing his teammates along in his ferocious
wake. And when LeBron goes down in the final
minute of the game, writhes on the court
in pain after landing on his wrist we all
want him to get up—even the artists rooting
for Golden State. *Get up, LeBron!* Nothing
comes easy to Cleveland. The next morning's
paper sports a photo of LeBron embracing
power forward Kevin Love, next to headlines
about Venezuelan food riots, triple-digit
temperatures in the West, vigils for
victims of the Orlando massacre, and
the Colorado woman who fought off
a mountain lion attacking her five-year-old
son—literally reached into the animal's
mouth and wrested his head from its jaws.
Too strong. In the belly of fear and rust

and shame there is no such thing.
To pry open something with your bare
hands, look into the gaping maw
of the beast that eats your sons—
the lion, the bullets, the streets, racist
cops, heroin, despair, whatever is most
predatory and say, *Enough—we will triumph,*
motherfuckers. At the game's end, LeBron
and the Cavs' coach Tyronn Lue sobbed
without shame. "I've always been tough
and never cried," Lue said. And LeBron
at the post-game mic, wearing a cut-down
net like a necklace says, "I came back to bring
a championship to our city. To a place
we've never been. We've got to get back
to Cleveland. We're going home."

Insane Flying Machines

What's in the box? Tonight's present contains
ten wings, ten tails, ten rudders, two fuselages
for assembly. We turn off NPR in the middle
of the train derailment story—four dead,
maybe faulty brakes to blame—and congregate
to bless the candles, which flare orange

and run wax rivers onto the counter, until
they eventually extinguish themselves
in delicate curls of smoke. Because the Gemara
says place the menorah next to a window
facing the street, we also twist the orange bulbs
of my grandmother's plastic electric on the sill,

left over from a time when plugs had two prongs,
which makes me nervous, since the local news
is all house fires and break-ins until Christmas.
The Gemara says in times of danger, placing
the menorah on a table indoors will suffice.
At Hanukkah we celebrate the Maccabees,

their victory over the forces of King Antiochus,
or the miracle of the temple oil lasting and lasting.
Danger includes all types of danger—the local
student who set himself on fire concocting
Butane hash oil, those people on the train.
What's in the box? Weary commuters

sleeping with ear buds, leaning their heads
against the windows on a Sunday while
a conductor works his way down the aisle
with his hole punch. What's in the box?

A metal xylophone and a yellow mallet.
Together they play music. Earlier today,

my son sits on my lap in a booth lined
in carpet while an audiologist—a woman
with very straight hair the color of butterscotch—
talks to him, makes boxes hung in each corner
light up when she says his name from one speaker
or the other. *Levi*, she says, again and again

into her microphone. Before his name was Levi,
it was King. What's in the box? Antiochus.
Us. We watch her lips through plexiglass,
but it's not clear if he can actually hear her words
from the right or left, though he looks sharply
when one speaker, for a moment, pops static.

In the next room the doctor tells me my son has fluid
behind both eardrums and says his son is adopted too,
from Utah, and he thought about naming his son
Utah, but his wife intervened. Interventions are,
by their very nature, dangerous: that train—
the news says some passengers were flung

from the windows. The news says the less wounded
helped the more seriously injured. One car nearly
went into the river, but it didn't. I do not want
my son to be put under, to get tubes in his ears.
He is scooting everywhere, takes four steps
at a clip, isn't yet a year, presses his small hand hard

to the lump that's grown above my breast and below
my voice box. My mother beat breast cancer
and now sees a meditation teacher at Memorial
Sloane Kettering to calm herself as part of their

holistic wellness program, but her practice does
not often calm her when she's on the phone

yelling, *If you visit that bitch, don't bother coming home,*
and then hangs up on me. She is talking about
my aunt, her dead-to-her sister, and when
I recount her anger to friends they counter
with tales of aunts and grandmothers who hold
similar vendettas—this fierceness that grows,

rather than dulls, with age. What's in the box?
An entire series of Captain Underpants books,
a Nerf Turbo Football, a keyboard made of electronic
flowers. My sister and I discuss my mother at length
behind closed doors, and every time, it ends in
what's in the box? The Holocaust, our grandmother's

time in the camps. The Gemara says danger includes
all types of danger, like gentiles stealing lights or
throwing stones. War, scarcity, oppression, darkness.
Hanukkah and Thanksgiving won't intersect again
for 76,000 years, and there are my sons—
the older assembling cardboard airplanes,

the younger pressing rainbow flowers which sound
notes of electronic joy. What's in the box? Anger
that does not dissipate with time. Chaos. Bubble wrap.
Hot Wheels. A plastic racing track. We are fine.
We are not fine. This holiday of miracles or war
or light, depending on the year, the spin.

Threat Assessment

is a violence prevention
strategy, says the online
document for school
administrators and crisis
teams, but the document
doesn't address what
I'm meant to do when
I open my email to find
a short note entitled
"Warning" that says
verbatim: *I am here to*
inform that in the next
couple of days I will break
into the campus and will
kill as many people as I can
until the police arrives.
The message is from
someone named Robert
Birdman, and when I
google him the first
hit is a photo of Robert
Franklin Stroud, the
"Birdman of Alcatraz,"
a federal prisoner who
was one of the most
notorious criminals
in US history and a
convicted murderer,
who also made important
contributions to avian
pathology while serving
a life sentence in solitary

confinement after finding
a nest with three injured
sparrows in a prison yard
in Leavenworth. My friend
Katie rehabilitates injured
turkey vultures—birds
considered scavengers
that feed exclusively
on carrion. When my
second son came to us
via adoption she sent
a stuffed turkey vulture
and a book with the birds
soaring alongside rhymed
text: *Wings stretch wide
to catch a ride on warming
air. Going where?* Around
the same time we began
reading to our new son,
police spotted circling
birds of prey above a
nearby farm and found
the remains of a college
student who had been
missing for months, used
DNA evidence to indict
a local man on charges
of abduction and murder.
Grainy video of the girl
on her last night alive
shows her running down
a hallway in a shiny gold
crop top, booking past
the Shell station on
Preston Avenue in the

dark. I know that part
of town, used to walk it
past midnight to visit a
guy I was sleeping with
in graduate school who
was maybe an addict
and played in a local
indie rock band. We
would sit on his porch
drinking beer and watch
the windowless patrol
wagon circle the block
and sometimes stop for
cops to load neighbors
into the back. What I've
left out is that we were
white and this neighbor-
hood was black. When
I went jogging at dusk,
one guy on his porch
would usually shout
white girl at me, and at
night helicopters circled
then landed at the hospital
up the block, painting
Nalle Street with sickly
vibrating light. In July
and August, you could
sometimes hear gun-
shots puncturing the
humidity. I've also
left out that the man
indicted for the murder
of the white female student
is black. The turkey vulture

lacks a syrinx—the vocal
organ of birds—which
means its only sounds
are grunts or low hisses.
Murderer Robert Stroud
was sent to Alcatraz after
guards discovered he had
been secretly making alcohol
in his cell. Stripped of his
birds, he wrote a history
of the penal system called
Looking Outward. Stroud
served 42 of his 54 years
in solitary confinement,
is considered the most famous
case of rehabilitation
and self-improvement in
an American prison. Each
year a turkey vulture raises
two chicks, which it feeds
by regurgitation. I have
two sons. My older son
is white and my younger
son is black. Colin
Kaepernick, once the
San Francisco 49ers
backup quarterback,
refused and still refuses
to stand for the national
anthem before games
in protest of wrongdoings
against African Americans
and minorities in this country.
One year, my older son,
who watches a lot of football

on television, added Colin
Kaepernick to the penciled
Christmas Cookie list I left
on the kitchen counter—
tucked his name between
Mr. Tom (school bus driver)
and Bridget (administrative
assistant). Kaepernick is
biracial, identifies as black,
and like my youngest son,
was adopted by a white
family when he was an
infant. The first time our
youngest son mentioned
the color of his skin
on his own was at the stables
where my mother took him
to ride ponies because
he's obsessed with them.
He pointed and said,
"That horse is brown
like me!" I have a shot
of him on the brown
horse in a blue helmet
with a serious expression
on his face. His helmet
is the same color as those
of the riot police I see
in every city, lined up
across from protesters
holding signs that say
No Justice / No Peace
or I Can't Breathe or
Black Lives Matter.
Once I discovered

the death threat email
from Robert Birdman
had gone to many others
on campus, I was relieved,
felt the bad grammar
meant it was a hoax
because who actually
gives warning of these
things, and what really
stops my heart is walking
past the open doors of
the massive auditorium
my husband lectures in
three times a week from
a raised stage to 500
students about principles
of microeconomics: supply
and demand, efficiency
and equity. How easy
it would be, how efficient,
for a lone gunman to
target that one room.
So when I receive a call
from my older son's
school which says,
"This is a test of the
Emergency Alert System—
all of our schools are
currently participating
in a lockdown drill," I
think of my son huddled
with the rest of his class
in a supply closet trying
to be quiet in the dark.
I have two sons, and

I can't protect either
of them from anything
at all. Colin Kaepernick
has many tattoos including
the words of Psalm 18:39—
you armed me with strength
for battle—and 27:3—
though a mighty army
surrounds me, my heart
will not fear. Those
injured sparrows
Robert Stroud found
in the Leavenworth
prison yard—he raised
them to adulthood.

Jackhammering Limestone

You ask about the leaves and I tell you it's been so dry here
the leaves are just giving up, turning brown, falling off the trees,

which all look dead. This might be a metaphor for the election or
might be a metaphor for nothing—it's hard to say. Each morning

I wake up to machines across the street jackhammering limestone,
shearing away more rock-face and turning it to rubble strewn across

red clay soil so dry it heaves and cracks. It's been seven weeks of
drilling and blasting, drilling and blasting, and that's not a metaphor

for anything either except maybe my mid-life crisis, which I'm having
surely as there's whiskey next to me and I'm up all night wondering

if I can be hairless again in some risqué places. Most days I refuse
to believe we're doomed, despite growing evidence to the contrary.

I mean, it's like the 1970s down there. Trust me. Most days, I listen
to NPR on my car radio and talk to one son or the other in the back seat

and ask them questions they sometimes answer as we drive home
past the pile of rubble and the leafless trees, which vaguely resemble

the girl I saw on campus wearing an entire shaggy outfit made from
flesh-colored plastic grocery bags campaigning on an environmental

platform for student council president. Her amazing bag-suit was rustling
in the breeze and it looked like she might take flight, just soar over campus

with the drones delivering burritos this week as a test stunt because
our motto here is *Invent the Future*, which I think about a lot—not as

'your future' in the sense of what I wanted to be when I grew up,
which I figured out by process of elimination was not a banker or a

computer programmer, and I never saw myself as a mother either but
here I am. More like I would invent a future where my black son will not

get shot by police for playing in a park, or driving, or walking from his
broken-down car. I would invent a future where there is always

enough chalk to leave notes for the next class: *We are starting a revolution*
somehow; instructions to follow. What no one told me about programming

computers for Merrill Lynch to keep their front-end trading systems
running past Y2K was that I was simply a dominatrix of code; the disaster

that would take our building down came later, and had nothing to do
with language. My cashier at Kroger has an epigraph on her name badge

under "Paula" that says, "I Will Make Things Right." I hope that girl
wins her election. I hope that someday someone else will enter my

hairless palace and find it marvelous. The photos of broken glass; the piles
of rubble. The future is throttling towards us and it's loud and reckless.

I'll Remember You as You Were,
Not as What You'll Become

If you are fearful, America,
I can tell you I am too. I worry
about my body—the way, lately,
it marches itself over curbs and
barriers, lingers in the streets
as a form of resistance.

The streets belong to no one
and everyone and are a guide
for motion, but we are so numerous
there is no pavement left on which to
release our bodies, like a river spilling
over a dam, so instead my body
thrums next to yours in place.

When we stop traffic or hold
hands to form a human chain,
we become a neon OPEN sign
singing into the night miles from
home when the only home left
is memory, your body, my body,
our scars, the dark punctuated
with the dying light of stars.

Notes

The titles of both "HolyMolyLand" poems come from visual artist Kim Beck's project called "Holymoley Land" (www.idealcities.com/holymoley-land).

The news articles cited in "HolyMolyLand" are "Austrian shepherd who drives refugees across border to safety" by Patrick Kingsley (*The Guardian*, 20 September 2015) and "Greek Hotel Owner on Refugees: 'These Could Have Been My Children'" by Kelly McEvers (NPR, 22 September 2015).

"Medium / Message" contains lines from Ezekiel 1:28.

"Double Sonnet Ending in New Testament" ends with lines from John 15:5.

The last line of "Elegy for the Body Before It's Released from Grief and into Light" is taken from photographer Barbara Ess writing on her own work in *I Am Not This Body* (Aperture, 2001).

The title "And Still We Gather with Infinite Momentum" comes from a photograph of the same name by Justin James King (www.justinjamesking.com).

The epigraph for the poem "DeSoto Park" is from Frank Stanford's poem "In Another Room I Am Drinking Eggs from a Boot" (poetryfoundation.org).

The title "What Follows Is a Reconstruction Based on the Best Available Evidence" comes from text in *Delirious New York* by Rem Koolhass (The Monacelli Press, 1997).

The title "No Matter How Many Skies Have Fallen" comes from a line in the first paragraph of *Lady Chatterley's Lover* by D.H. Lawrence (Bantam Books, 1983).

"The Clock of the Long Now" is a proposed mechanical clock designed to keep time for 10,000 years. The phrase "The Long Now" originally comes from an essay by Brian Eno called "The Big Here and the Long Now."

The title "But My Heart Is Wild and My Bones Are Steel" comes from Phosphorescent's lyrics in "Song for Zula" via Patte Loper's artwork of the same name (www.patteloper.com).

The title "Your Rivers, Your Margins, Your Diminutive Villages" is from visual artist Patte Loper's exhibit and works of the same name.

Some phrases from "Poem with Warehouse Fire & Disaster Recovery Team" are taken from a newspaper article entitled "Fire at a Brooklyn Warehouse Puts Private Lives on Display" by Vivian Yee (*The New York Times*, 1 Feb 2015).

Some lines in "*Too strong*" are taken from "Cavaliers Defeat Warriors to Win Their First NBA Title" by Scott Cacciola (*The New York Times*, 19 June 2016).

Lines in "Threat Assessment" come from *Vulture View* by April Sayre (Henry Holt & Co., 2007), and "Colin Kaepernick Stands Up by Sitting Down for Anthem" by Robert Klemko (*The MMQB*, 27 August 2016).

The title "I'll Remember You as You Were, Not as What You'll Become" is from visual artist Sky Hopinka's work of the same name (www.skyhopinka.com).

Acknowledgments

I am grateful to all the editors of the following journals and anthologies where these poems, sometimes in different form or with different titles, first appeared:

The Ampersand Review: "Factography: Hometown," "Loss Prevention Starts with You," "But My Heart Is Wild and My Bones Are Steel";

Apalachee Review: "Austerity";

At Length: "Medium / Message";

Bennington Review: "Peregrinus";

Colorado Review: "Hat Trick";

Columbia Poetry Review: "Threat Assessment";

Copper Nickel: "Insane Flying Machines";

Crab Orchard Review: "Your Rivers, Your Margins, Your Diminutive Villages";

Forklift, Ohio: A Journal of Poetry, Cooking & Light Industrial Safety: "And Still We Gather with Infinite Momentum" (as "Funkchance");

Fourth Genre: "HolyMolyLand";

HEArt: "No Matter How Many Skies Have Fallen";

The Kenyon Review: "On the Road," "Post-Game-Day Blessing";

Kestrel: "Our Holiday Letter";

Love's Executive Order: "I'll Remember You as You Were, Not as What You'll Become";

Oxford American: "Dollar General";

Ploughshares: "Poem with Warehouse Fire & Disaster Recovery Team";

Plume: "Double Sonnet Ending in New Testament";

Poetry Northwest: "The Clock of the Long Now";

Puerto del Sol: "Images from the Archives of the Institute for Esoteric Research";

Shenandoah: "Continuation";

Southern Indiana Review: "What Follows Is a Reconstruction Based on the Best Available Evidence" (as "anything that wasn't a dugong");

The Southern Review: "Elegy for the Body Before It's Released from Grief and into Light" (as "Another Ohio Road Trip");

Territory: "HolyMolyLand";
Tin House: "Jackhammering Limestone";
Virginia Quarterly Review: "Too strong."

"Diaspora" was first published in *The Plume Anthology of Poetry 3*, Ed. Daniel Lawless (MadHat Press, 2015).

"Post-Game-Day Blessing" was reprinted in *The Book of Uncommon Prayer*, Ed. Matthew Vollmer (Outpost19, 2015).

"I'll Remember You as You Were, Not as What You'll Become" also appeared as part of *22 Steps* (Stair Installation) at the Moss Arts Center at Virginia Tech (April–August 2017).

• • •

Thanks to Virginia Tech's English Department, College of Liberal Arts and Human Sciences, and Center for the Arts for research support that enabled me to write these poems. I am grateful to the US-UK Fulbright Commission for my time in Northern Ireland, and to the 2015 faculty and students at the Seamus Heaney Centre for Poetry at Queen's University Belfast for their community and camaraderie. I am indebted to the MacDowell Colony and the Virginia Center for the Creative Arts for time and space. To the poets who read these poems and offered their skills and wisdom: Sandra Beasley, Mary Biddinger, Conor Bracken, Jenny Browne, Jehanne Dubrow, Carmen Giménez Smith, Matthew Guenette, Joy Katz, Danielle Pafunda, David Stack, Marcela Sulak, Rachel Zucker, and especially the ever-fabulous Keetje Kuipers—I don't even know how to thank you enough. Praise to my electronic poem-a-day groups, in your ever-shifting compositions, for keeping me accountable—you know who you are. This book would never have been written if it weren't for the staff of the Child Development Center for Learning and Research at Virginia Tech, who joyfully cared for and educated my children over the past ten years. Thanks to Nat Jacks at Inkwell Management, and to the amazing team at BOA Editions: Peter, Ron, Kelly—and also to Sandy and Richard for their artistry and wizardry. Immeasurable gratitude goes to my kids, who have to put up with their weird poet-mama in perpetuity, and to my partner-in-crime, Steve Trost, who's always made space for my work, even when I wasn't able to. Levi, we waited for you for so long—this book is for you.

About the Author

Erika Meitner is the author of the poetry collections *Copia*, *Ideal Cities* (a National Poetry Series winner), *Makeshift Instructions for Vigilant Girls*, and *Inventory at the All-night Drugstore*. Meitner's poems have been anthologized widely, and have appeared in publications including *Tin House*, *Virginia Quarterly Review*, *The New York Times Magazine*, *Ploughshares*, *The New Republic*, and *Oxford American*. She has received fellowships from the MacDowell Colony, the Wisconsin Institute for Creative Writing, the Virginia Center for the Creative Arts, and Blue Mountain Center, and she was the 2015 US-UK Fulbright Distinguished Scholar in Creative Writing at the Seamus Heaney Centre for Poetry at Queen's University Belfast. She is currently an associate professor of English at Virginia Tech, where she directs the MFA and undergraduate programs in Creative Writing.

BOA Editions, Ltd. American Poets Continuum Series

No. 1 *The Fuhrer Bunker: A Cycle of Poems in Progress*
W. D. Snodgrass

No. 2 *She*
M. L. Rosenthal

No. 3 *Living With Distance*
Ralph J. Mills, Jr.

No. 4 *Not Just Any Death*
Michael Waters

No. 5 *That Was Then: New and Selected Poems*
Isabella Gardner

No. 6 *Things That Happen Where There Aren't Any People*
William Stafford

No. 7 *The Bridge of Change: Poems 1974–1980*
John Logan

No. 8 *Signatures*
Joseph Stroud

No. 9 *People Live Here: Selected Poems 1949–1983*
Louis Simpson

No. 10 *Yin*
Carolyn Kizer

No. 11 *Duhamel: Ideas of Order in Little Canada*
Bill Tremblay

No. 12 *Seeing It Was So*
Anthony Piccione

No. 13 *Hyam Plutzik: The Collected Poems*

No. 14 *Good Woman: Poems and a Memoir 1969–1980*
Lucille Clifton

No. 15 *Next: New Poems*
Lucille Clifton

No. 16 *Roxa: Voices of the Culver Family*
William B. Patrick

No. 17 *John Logan: The Collected Poems*

No. 18 *Isabella Gardner: The Collected Poems*

No. 19 *The Sunken Lightship*
Peter Makuck

No. 20 *The City in Which I Love You*
Li-Young Lee

No. 21 *Quilting: Poems 1987–1990*
Lucille Clifton

No. 22 *John Logan: The Collected Fiction*

No. 23 *Shenandoah and Other Verse Plays*
Delmore Schwartz

No. 24 *Nobody Lives on Arthur Godfrey Boulevard*
Gerald Costanzo

No. 25 *The Book of Names: New and Selected Poems*
Barton Sutter

No. 26 *Each in His Season*
W. D. Snodgrass

No. 27 *Wordworks: Poems Selected and New*
Richard Kostelanetz

No. 28 *What We Carry*
Dorianne Laux

No. 29 *Red Suitcase*
Naomi Shihab Nye

No. 30 *Song*
Brigit Pegeen Kelly

No. 31 *The Fuehrer Bunker: The Complete Cycle*
W. D. Snodgrass

No. 32 *For the Kingdom*
Anthony Piccione

No. 33 *The Quicken Tree*
Bill Knott

No. 34 *These Upraised Hands*
William B. Patrick

No. 35 *Crazy Horse in Stillness*
William Heyen

No. 36 *Quick, Now, Always*
Mark Irwin

No. 37 *I Have Tasted the Apple*
Mary Crow

No. 38 *The Terrible Stories*
Lucille Clifton

No. 39 *The Heat of Arrivals*
Ray Gonzalez

No. 40 *Jimmy & Rita*
Kim Addonizio

No. 41 *Green Ash, Red Maple, Black Gum*
Michael Waters

No. 42 *Against Distance*
Peter Makuck

No. 43 *The Night Path*
Laurie Kutchins

No. 44 *Radiography*
Bruce Bond

No. 45 *At My Ease: Uncollected Poems
of the Fifties and Sixties*
David Ignatow

No. 46 *Trillium*
Richard Foerster

No. 47 *Fuel*
Naomi Shihab Nye

No. 48 *Gratitude*
Sam Hamill

No. 49 *Diana, Charles, & the Queen*
William Heyen

No. 50 *Plus Shipping*
Bob Hicok

No. 51 *Cabato Sentora*
Ray Gonzalez

No. 52 *We Didn't Come Here for This*
William B. Patrick

No. 53 *The Vandals*
Alan Michael Parker

No. 54 *To Get Here*
Wendy Mnookin

No. 55 *Living Is What I Wanted: Last Poems*
David Ignatow

No. 56 *Dusty Angel*
Michael Blumenthal

No. 57 *The Tiger Iris*
Joan Swift

No. 58 *White City*
Mark Irwin

No. 59 *Laugh at the End of the World:
Collected Comic Poems 1969–1999*
Bill Knott

No. 60 *Blessing the Boats: New and
Selected Poems: 1988–2000*
Lucille Clifton

No. 61 *Tell Me*
Kim Addonizio

No. 62 *Smoke*
Dorianne Laux

No. 63 *Parthenopi: New and Selected Poems*
Michael Waters

No. 64 *Rancho Notorious*
Richard Garcia

No. 65 *Jam*
Joe-Anne McLaughlin

No. 66 *A. Poulin, Jr. Selected Poems*
Edited, with an Introduction
by Michael Waters

No. 67 *Small Gods of Grief*
Laure-Anne Bosselaar

No. 68 *Book of My Nights*
Li-Young Lee

No. 69 *Tulip Farms and Leper Colonies*
Charles Harper Webb

No. 70 *Double Going*
Richard Foerster

No. 71 *What He Took*
Wendy Mnookin

No. 72 *The Hawk Temple at Tierra Grande*
Ray Gonzalez

No. 73 *Mules of Love*
Ellen Bass

No. 74 *The Guests at the Gate*
Anthony Piccione

No. 75 *Dumb Luck*
Sam Hamill

No. 76 *Love Song with Motor Vehicles*
Alan Michael Parker

No. 77 *Life Watch*
Willis Barnstone

No. 78 *The Owner of the House: New
Collected Poems 1940–2001*
Louis Simpson

No. 79   *Is*
Wayne Dodd

No. 80   *Late*
Cecilia Woloch

No. 81   *Precipitates*
Debra Kang Dean

No. 82   *The Orchard*
Brigit Pegeen Kelly

No. 83   *Bright Hunger*
Mark Irwin

No. 84   *Desire Lines: New and Selected Poems*
Lola Haskins

No. 85   *Curious Conduct*
Jeanne Marie Beaumont

No. 86   *Mercy*
Lucille Clifton

No. 87   *Model Homes*
Wayne Koestenbaum

No. 88   *Farewell to the Starlight in Whiskey*
Barton Sutter

No. 89   *Angels for the Burning*
David Mura

No. 90   *The Rooster's Wife*
Russell Edson

No. 91   *American Children*
Jim Simmerman

No. 92   *Postcards from the Interior*
Wyn Cooper

No. 93   *You & Yours*
Naomi Shihab Nye

No. 94   *Consideration of the Guitar:
New and Selected Poems 1986–2005*
Ray Gonzalez

No. 95   *Off-Season in the Promised Land*
Peter Makuck

No. 96   *The Hoopoe's Crown*
Jacqueline Osherow

No. 97   *Not for Specialists:
New and Selected Poems*
W. D. Snodgrass

No. 98   *Splendor*
Steve Kronen

No. 99   *Woman Crossing a Field*
Deena Linett

No. 100   *The Burning of Troy*
Richard Foerster

No. 101   *Darling Vulgarity*
Michael Waters

No. 102   *The Persistence of Objects*
Richard Garcia

No. 103   *Slope of the Child Everlasting*
Laurie Kutchins

No. 104   *Broken Hallelujahs*
Sean Thomas Dougherty

No. 105   *Peeping Tom's Cabin:
Comic Verse 1928–2008*
X. J. Kennedy

No. 106   *Disclamor*
G.C. Waldrep

No. 107   *Encouragement for a Man
Falling to His Death*
Christopher Kennedy

No. 108   *Sleeping with Houdini*
Nin Andrews

No. 109   *Nomina*
Karen Volkman

No. 110   *The Fortieth Day*
Kazim Ali

No. 111   *Elephants & Butterflies*
Alan Michael Parker

No. 112   *Voices*
Lucille Clifton

No. 113   *The Moon Makes Its Own Plea*
Wendy Mnookin

No. 114   *The Heaven-Sent Leaf*
Katy Lederer

No. 115   *Struggling Times*
Louis Simpson

No. 116   *And*
Michael Blumenthal

No. 117   *Carpathia*
Cecilia Woloch

No. 118   *Seasons of Lotus, Seasons of Bone*
Matthew Shenoda

No. 119   *Sharp Stars*
Sharon Bryan

No. 120   *Cool Auditor*
Ray Gonzalez

No. 121 *Long Lens: New and Selected Poems*
Peter Makuck

No. 122 *Chaos Is the New Calm*
Wyn Cooper

No. 123 *Diwata*
Barbara Jane Reyes

No. 124 *Burning of the Three Fires*
Jeanne Marie Beaumont

No. 125 *Sasha Sings the Laundry on the Line*
Sean Thomas Dougherty

No. 126 *Your Father on the Train of Ghosts*
G.C. Waldrep and John Gallaher

No. 127 *Ennui Prophet*
Christopher Kennedy

No. 128 *Transfer*
Naomi Shihab Nye

No. 129 *Gospel Night*
Michael Waters

No. 130 *The Hands of Strangers: Poems from the Nursing Home*
Janice N. Harrington

No. 131 *Kingdom Animalia*
Aracelis Girmay

No. 132 *True Faith*
Ira Sadoff

No. 133 *The Reindeer Camps and Other Poems*
Barton Sutter

No. 134 *The Collected Poems of Lucille Clifton: 1965–2010*

No. 135 *To Keep Love Blurry*
Craig Morgan Teicher

No. 136 *Theophobia*
Bruce Beasley

No. 137 *Refuge*
Adrie Kusserow

No. 138 *The Book of Goodbyes*
Jillian Weise

No. 139 *Birth Marks*
Jim Daniels

No. 140 *No Need of Sympathy*
Fleda Brown

No. 141 *There's a Box in the Garage You Can Beat with a Stick*
Michael Teig

No. 142 *The Keys to the Jail*
Keetje Kuipers

No. 143 *All You Ask for Is Longing: New and Selected Poems 1994–2014*
Sean Thomas Dougherty

No. 144 *Copia*
Erika Meitner

No. 145 *The Chair: Prose Poems*
Richard Garcia

No. 146 *In a Landscape*
John Gallaher

No. 147 *Fanny Says*
Nickole Brown

No. 148 *Why God Is a Woman*
Nin Andrews

No. 149 *Testament*
G.C. Waldrep

No. 150 *I'm No Longer Troubled by the Extravagance*
Rick Bursky

No. 151 *Antidote for Night*
Marsha de la O

No. 152 *Beautiful Wall*
Ray Gonzalez

No. 153 *the black maria*
Aracelis Girmay

No. 154 *Celestial Joyride*
Michael Waters

No. 155 *Whereso*
Karen Volkman

No. 156 *The Day's Last Light Reddens the Leaves of the Copper Beech*
Stephen Dobyns

No. 157 *The End of Pink*
Kathryn Nuernberger

No. 158 *Mandatory Evacuation*
Peter Makuck

No. 159 *Primitive: The Art and Life of Horace H. Pippin*
Janice N. Harrington

No. 160 *The Trembling Answers*
Craig Morgan Teicher

No. 161 *Bye-Bye Land*
Christian Barter

No. 162 *Sky Country*
Christine Kitano

No. 163 *All Soul Parts Returned*
Bruce Beasley

No. 164 *The Smoke of Horses*
Charles Rafferty

No. 165 *The Second O of Sorrow*
Sean Thomas Dougherty

No. 166 *Holy Moly Carry Me*
Erika Meitner

Colophon

BOA Editions, Ltd., a not-for-profit publisher of poetry and other literary works, fosters readership and appreciation of contemporary literature. By identifying, cultivating, and publishing both new and established poets and selecting authors of unique literary talent, BOA brings high-quality literature to the public. Support for this effort comes from the sale of its publications, grant funding, and private donations.

• • •

*The publication of this book is made possible, in part,
by the support of the following individuals:*

Anonymous
Jeanne Marie Beaumont
Angela Bonazinga & Catherine Lewis
Helen Burnham
Gwen & Gary Conners
Robert & Rae Gilson
Gouvernet Arts Fund
Melissa Hall & Joe Torre
Sandi Henschel, *in honor of Boo Poulin*
Chalonda Roberts James
Jack & Gail Langerak
Marcia Lowry
Joe McElveney
Boo Poulin, *in honor of Sandi Henschel*
Boo Poulin
Robert Thomas
Deborah Ronnen & Sherman Levey
Steven O. Russell & Phyllis Rifkin-Russell
Allan & Melanie Ulrich
William Waddell & Linda Rubel
William Waddell & Linda Rubel, *in honor of Simah, Ethan, and Jeehye*
Michael Waters & Mihaela Moscaliuc